WELCOME TO MY COUNTRY

Welcome to
CANADA

Gareth Stevens Publishing
MILWAUKEE

JUN 2008

Written by
BOB BARLAS and **NORMAN TOMPSETT/SUSAN MCKAY**

Designed by
SHARIFAH FAUZIAH

Picture research by
SUSAN JANE MANUEL

First published in North America in 1999 by
Gareth Stevens Publishing
1555 North RiverCenter Drive, Suite 201
Milwaukee, Wisconsin 53212 USA

For a free color catalog describing
Gareth Stevens Publishing's list of high-quality books
and multimedia programs, call
1-800-542-2595 (USA) or
1-800-461-9120 (CANADA)
Gareth Stevens Publishing's
Fax: (414) 225-0377.

© **TIMES EDITIONS PTE LTD 1999**
Originated and designed by
Times Books International
an imprint of Times Editions Pte Ltd
Times Centre, 1 New Industrial Road
Singapore 536196
http://www.timesone.com.sg/te

Library of Congress Cataloging-in-Publication Data
Barlas, Robert.
Welcome to Canada / Bob Barlas, Norman Tompsett,
and Susan McKay.
p. cm. — (Welcome to my country)
Includes bibliographical references and index.
Summary: An overview of the geography, history, government,
economy, people, and culture of Canada.
ISBN 0-8368-2394-X (lib.bdg.)
1. Canada—Juvenile literature. [1. Canada.]
I. Tompsett, Norm. II. McKay, Susan, 1972– .
III. Title. IV. Series.
F1008.2.B38 1999
971-dc21   99-18320

Printed in Malaysia

1 2 3 4 5 6 7 8 9 03 02 01 00 99

PICTURE CREDITS
Axiom Photographic Agency: 40
Bes Stock, 3 (top), 23, 30 (bottom)
Camera Press Ltd: 15, 29 (right), 32
Canada-ASEAN Centre: 25 (bottom),
    29 (left)
Canada Tourism Commission/Excel Images:
    13, 17, 31, 33 (top), 35, 38
CanaPress Photo Service: 37
Communauté urbaine de Quebec–
    Communications: 6 (bottom)
Jane Cox: 7
Crombie, McNeill: 16 (top)
Focus Team–Italy: 41
Winston Fraser: 12 (bottom)
Dave G. Houser: 6 (top), 20
Hutchison Library: 5, 16 (bottom), 19
Industry Canada: cover, 3 (center), 8, 9 (top),
    34, 36, 39
Life File: cover, 12 (top), 22
Photobank Photolibrary/Singapore: 2, 45
David Simson: 24, 28
Times Editions: 33 (bottom)
Topham Picturepoint: 4, 10, 11, 14, 25 (top)
Travel Ink: 21
Trip Photographic Library: 1, 3 (bottom), 9
    (bottom), 18, 26, 27, 30 (top)

Digital Scanning by Superskill Graphics Pte Ltd

Contents

5 **Welcome to Canada!**

6 **The Land**

10 **History**

16 **Government and the Economy**

20 **People and Lifestyle**

28 **Language**

30 **Arts**

34 **Leisure**

40 **Food**

42 **Map**

44 **Quick Facts**

46 **Glossary**

47 **Books, Videos, Web Sites**

48 **Index**

Words that appear in the glossary are printed in **boldface** type the first time they occur in the text.

Welcome to Canada!

Canada is a beautiful country. With mountains, prairies, waterfalls, and lakes, it is a wonderful place for nature lovers. There is a great mixture of people in Canada from countries all over the world. Join us as we learn about Canadians and their amazing country.

Below: More than one million people emigrated to Canada between 1991 and 1997. Today, Mandarin (a Chinese **dialect**) is the third-most common language, after English and French.

Opposite: Canada geese rest in the winter snow.

The Flag of Canada

The maple leaf is Canada's national symbol. It has twelve points. The red stripes on either side of the flag represent two oceans — the Pacific Ocean and the Atlantic Ocean.

The Land

Canada is the second largest country in the world. It stretches from the island of Newfoundland in the east to the territory of Yukon in the west. It is bordered by the lower forty-eight states of the United States to the south and Alaska to the west. Canada is divided into eleven provinces and three territories. Although it is a huge country, its population is only one-third that of the United States.

Above: Niagara Falls lies on the border between Canada and the United States.

Canada has seven separate regions. In the east are hills and valleys. The center is covered in a sheet of ancient rock called the Canadian Shield. Farther west, in the Great Plains, the land is wide and flat. West of this lie the Rocky Mountains, the Cariboo Mountains, and the Coastal Mountains.

In the Arctic Lowlands, the ground is swampy, with low-growing trees. The northern coast includes many small islands, cliffs, and **fjords**.

Above: The Rocky Mountains stretch from Canada, south through the United States, and down to Mexico.

Opposite, bottom: The Chute-Montmorency Falls in Quebec are higher than Niagara Falls. In winter, they freeze and become a popular place for tobogganing.

Seasons

Spring is a beautiful time of year in Canada. Bright green leaves appear, and flowers bloom. Summer is usually hot. This is when many Canadians go to the beach or vacation at a lake. Leaves begin to change

color and fall from trees in autumn. Winter is coldest in the northern and central plains. Snow covers most of the country from late November to the middle of March.

Above: Leaves turn brilliant shades of red, orange, and yellow in autumn.

Plants and Animals

The beaver is a national symbol of Canada. It makes its home near lakes. The moose is one of Canada's largest animals. Other animals, such as chipmunks, raccoons, and groundhogs, also make their homes in Canada. The most famous bird is the Canada goose.

Plants have learned to adapt to the climate in Canada. Alpine plants, such as juniper or lichen, grow close to the ground to avoid the cold and wind. Prairie plants have long roots to help them reach in the earth for water.

Above: This trillium flower is one of the first signs of spring in Canada.

Left: The Arctic fox lives in northern parts of Canada. Its white fur helps **camouflage** it in the snow.

History

In early times, small groups of native tribes from Asia lived in western and central Canada. The first white people to reach North America were the **Vikings** from Iceland and Greenland. Leif Ericson, called "Eric the Red," landed on the tip of Newfoundland around A.D. 1000. Many native Indians and **Inuit** still live in Canada today. The Vikings did not set up permanent **colonies** there.

Above: Today, Samuel de Champlain is sometimes called "The Father of Canada."

Early Explorers

The first explorers who did set up colonies came to Canada from England and France. In 1605, Frenchman Samuel de Champlain founded Port Royal (now called Annapolis Royal), the first European settlement in North America, in the province of Nova Scotia.

French-English Rivalry

The French who came to Canada were interested in the fur trade more than anything else. In those days, fur was almost as valuable as gold.

The British set up special fur trading companies in competition with the French. Soon, the **rivalry** grew and war broke out. In 1760, the French lost an important battle at the Plains of Abraham. In 1763, a **treaty** was signed in Paris forcing the French to give up their Canadian colonies to the British.

Below: Fur trading was an important business in Canada in the seventeenth and eighteenth centuries.

Forming a Nation

In 1867, the Dominion of Canada was formed, and Sir John A. MacDonald became prime minister. In 1871, he decided to build a coast-to-coast railway. This upset the **Métis** people of the west, who wanted to protect their land. They started two **rebellions**, led by Louis Riel. When the railroad was completed, soldiers reached the area to fight the rebellion. After he lost the fight, Riel was tried and hanged.

Above: In 1873, the North-West Mounted Police was formed to patrol central, northern, and western Canada. Today, they are known as The Mounties.

Completing the Country

In 1896, gold was discovered in the Yukon. This sparked a gold rush. One hundred thousand people flocked to the Klondike gold fields to make their fortune. Two years later, the Yukon became a territory.

In 1905, the new provinces of Saskatchewan and Alberta were created on the Great Plains. In 1949, Newfoundland became Canada's tenth province.

Above: Tourists in the Yukon can relive the days of the gold rush by panning for gold.

Opposite, bottom: The grave of Louis Riel stands in Batoche National Historic Park in Saskatchewan.

Government and the Economy

Government

The Canadian federal government is responsible for national affairs, such as the environment and defense. Each province has a government, which looks after education and health. Governments in towns and cities are responsible for day-to-day affairs.

Above: "The changing of the guard" at the Parliament in Ottawa (**below**).

The Canadian Parliament has two houses — the House of Commons and the Senate. Members of the House of Commons are elected every four or five years. Members of the House propose laws. The Senate, made up of senators appointed by the prime minister, reviews the **proposals**. If the proposals are approved, bills go to the governor general for his or her signature, after which they become laws.

Above: Canada's eleventh province, Nunavut, was established in 1999. It is governed by the Inuit. In their language, *Nunavut* means "our land."

Industry

Manufacturing is the largest industry in Canada. Canada manufactures automobiles and forest products for **export**. Canada's biggest trading partner is the United States. The two countries trade products freely through NAFTA (North American Free Trade Agreement). Trade with the European Union and Asia Pacific is growing quickly.

Above: Trees are manufactured into paper at pulp mills like this one.

Resources

Canada is one of the world's biggest producers of grain. Most of the grain grows in the prairie provinces of Manitoba, Saskatchewan, and Alberta. Fishing is also important, but recently, the supply of fish has begun to decline. Canada has vast reserves of oil and natural gas, minerals (such as nickel, potash, silver, and gold), and forested areas.

Below: Harvest time in Alberta. Golden bales of hay are cut and rolled before being hauled away.

People and Lifestyle

A Mosaic of People

Canada is home to many different peoples, customs, languages, and religions. Many people living in each province descend from the same place. So, many Canadians living in Nova Scotia are **descendants** of the original native people — the Micmac Indians. Many people of French descent live in New Brunswick.

Below: The Inuit can be recognized by their Asian features. About 21,000 Inuit live in Canada.

As well as being home to native Canadians, Ontario is also home to large groups of people from many different ethnic backgrounds. The majority of people living in Quebec are descendants of the French. British Columbia is home to Brits and Chinese. Alberta, Manitoba, and Saskatchewan were settled by many European **immigrants**.

Above: Vancouver has one of the largest Chinese communities in North America.

The Family Home

It is important to Canadians to own their own homes. Most houses in Canada are built from a wooden frame filled with **insulating material** to keep out the cold. Around this frame is an outer layer of brick or vinyl that gives the house its distinct look. Some Canadians own a home in the city and another in the country, for relaxing weekend vacations.

Above: A typical Canadian home in the city.

Houses generally have two to four bedrooms, a kitchen, a living room, and one or two bathrooms. Some houses in the countryside are so far apart that people cannot see their neighbor's house.

Not all Canadians live in houses — many live in apartments. Cities usually have large apartment complexes with facilities such as swimming pools and tennis courts.

Below: An apartment complex in Montreal, Quebec.

Education

More than 90 percent of students in Canada go to public schools. Starting at three or four years of age, children attend day-care or nursery school. Elementary school runs from kindergarten through sixth grade or eighth grade; junior high school from grades seven to eight; and high school from grades nine to twelve (or grade eleven in Quebec).

Opposite: Many students can attend a university **lecture.** University classes are much bigger than high school ones.

Below: A preschool outing to Toronto's city hall.

After graduation, students can go to community colleges, technical colleges, or universities. Courses at community colleges teach students practical skills, such as nursing, police work, and journalism. Coursework takes two or three years to complete, and the student receives a diploma. University courses last for three or four years and award students with a degree. Canada has many good universities.

Above: Terry Fox is a national hero who tried to run across Canada to raise money for cancer research. The Terry Fox Centre gives money to students to work on various projects.

Religion

The native people of Canada believe spirits dwell in nature, so they treat all of nature with a special respect. When the French and English arrived in North America, they did not know about the religion of the natives. European missionaries came to **convert** the people to Christianity. They tried to teach the native people to be good Christians by praying to God.

Below: The French settlers of Canada were Catholics. This is one of the many Catholic churches the French built in Quebec. It is the Notre Dame Cathedral in Montreal.

Above: A Sikh gurudwara, or place of worship, in Toronto.

Many natives still follow their original beliefs. As more and more different types of people come to Canada, more religions have been introduced. Immigrants from Asia brought Buddhism, Hinduism, Sikhism, and Islam.

Today, all across the country, mosques, temples, and synagogues exist and flourish alongside the cathedrals and churches built by early Christian settlers.

Language

Canada has two official languages — French and English. All students study both languages. Many other languages are spoken in Canada, including Mandarin, Vietnamese, and Hindi. Students can attend special classes to learn other languages, such as Polish or Arabic.

Above: In 1969, Canada became bilingual. Two national languages now exist — English and French.

Distinctly Canadian

Canadian English is different from American English. Canadians have kept many of the British spellings, for example, "colour" and "centre," and pronunciation is slightly different. Canadian French is also very different from the French spoken in Europe. The original French settlers came from throughout France and spoke many different **dialects**.

Literature

Canadian literature grew from the folktales and stories of the early settlers. The most well-known French-Canadian writer is probably Gabrielle Roy, who won the *Prix Femina*. Michael Ondaatje and Margaret Atwood are two well-known English-Canadian writers. Canadian Lucy Maud Montgomery made *Anne of Green Gables* famous in her books set on Prince Edward Island. The native people have many tales and myths, but few are written down.

Below, left: Michael Ondaatje won the Booker Prize for *The English Patient* in 1992.

Below, right: Margaret Atwood has written several books, including *Cat's Eye* and *A Handmaid's Tale*.

Arts

The Inuit, the people of northern Canada, are famous for their **soapstone** carvings. Arctic scenes and animals, such as polar bears, seals, and whales, are popular subjects. Totem poles provide another example of native art.

Above: An Inuit soapstone sculpture by artist Mary Oshutsiaq.

Artist Emily Carr painted the Indians and landscape of British Columbia. The most famous artists from Canada are called the Group of

Left: The National Gallery in Ottawa features exhibitions of famous Canadian artists.

Seven. They produced paintings of the beautiful Canadian landscape in the 1920s.

Above: The Place des Arts in Quebec has five huge halls. It is the most important center for the performing arts in Canada.

Theater is very popular in Canada. The Stratford Festival is a huge theater production in Ontario honoring William Shakespeare. Many big cities have professional theater companies that stage musicals and plays. Montreal is home to the National Theater School, where aspiring young actors train.

Music

Canadian music is derived from many different styles: Jamaican reggae, African-American rap, Celtic folk music, and French **ballads**. Popular rock stars include Celine Dion, Bryan Adams, Shania Twain, k. d. lang, Joni Mitchell, and Alanis Morisette.

Opposite: One of Canada's most famous ballet companies is The Royal Winnipeg Ballet.

Left: Bryan Adams is famous around the world for his love songs and hard rock style.

Dance

Canadians enjoy dancing, whatever form it might take. Across Canada, young people master everything from Scottish highland dances to the intricate steps of classical Indian dance. Every year, well-known ballet companies, such as the National Ballet and Royal Winnipeg Ballet, present world-class shows. They are also popular around the world and travel to other countries to perform.

Above: Singer Anne Murray has won four Grammys and two American Music Awards.

Leisure

The Great Outdoors

Canadians have a great love of the outdoors. Camping sites exist in almost every part of the country. With its many lakes, forests, and mountains, Canada is a nature lover's paradise. In winter, cross-country and downhill skiing are popular sports. The slopes are never far away. Snowmobiles and skidoos are favorite vehicles to travel around on.

Below: Some of the best skiing in the world can be found in the Canadian Rockies.

Relaxing Indoors

Indoor leisure pursuits are just as popular with Canadians as outdoor ones. Surfing the Internet, going to the movies, and playing Nintendo are a few favorites. Some people enjoy collecting antiques, building model railroads, or playing card games.

Canadians also enjoy all kinds of crafts. In the summer months, local craftspeople display their work at shows and exhibitions.

Above: Flea markets are popular places to visit on the weekend to find wonderful antiques at bargain prices.

Hockey

Many Canadians learn to play ice hockey as small children. Young boys dream of playing in the National Hockey League (NHL) one day. Many people spend Saturday nights watching television's "Hockey Night in Canada," when the NHL games are broadcast. Almost every neighborhood has an ice rink, where children and adults play hockey after school and work, and on weekends.

Below: Hockey can sometimes be a very dangerous game. Players wear padding and helmets to protect themselves if they fall or get hit.

Other Sports

The oldest Canadian game is lacrosse. Lacrosse originated from a native game called *baggataway* (ba-gat-teh-WAY).

Recently, Canada has become known for its track and field athletes. The record for the 100-meter sprint is now held by Canadian Donovan Bailey. He set the record at the 1996 Atlanta Summer Olympics.

Above, left:
Donovan Bailey is the fastest man in the world. He ran the 100-meter sprint in 9.84 seconds.

Above, right:
Canadian diver Anne Pelletier won a bronze medal at the Atlanta Olympic Games in 1996.

Canada Day

July 1 marks Canada Day, celebrating the birth of the Dominion of Canada in 1867. In Ottawa, Ontario, the prime minister makes a speech and gives a special award to new citizens. Parades and picnics take place during the day, and there are fireworks at night. Some people dress in special costumes. In 1992, Canada celebrated its 125th birthday.

Below: On Canada Day, fairs, carnivals, and picnics are held. People eat, drink, play games, and even get their faces painted!

The Calgary Stampede

Every year in July, Calgary, Alberta, hosts the Calgary Stampede. It is the biggest rodeo in the world! Cowboys gather to tame wild horses and fierce bulls. They also wrestle with young cattle, throw lassos, and race horse-drawn **chuckwagons**. The Calgary Stampede lasts ten days. Other events include pancake breakfasts, square dancing, colorful parades, and special western music performances.

Above: Chuckwagon racing was invented at the Calgary Stampede in 1925. Cowboys load tent poles and a box or barrel onto the chuckwagon and race around a difficult track.

Food

Canadian food is a mixture of tastes from all over the world. Dishes from Italy, Greece, and China can be found alongside native foods, such as Saskatoon berries, **fiddleheads**, and maple syrup.

Left: Prince Edward Island is the home of the Canadian lobster. Even McDonald's restaurants have a lobster burger on the menu when lobsters are in season.

Distinctive Dishes

Canada has some very distinctive dishes. Seal flipper pies, made with seal blubber and pork, come from Newfoundland. In New Brunswick, fiddleheads are popular. In Quebec, *tortiere* (tor-tee-EHR) is served on Christmas Eve. And the Saskatoon berry, from Saskatchewan, is used in pies. But the most famous Canadian food is maple syrup. Throughout Canada, it is poured over pancakes and used to flavor ice cream.

Above: Pouring hot maple syrup over snow makes it turn hard and crunchy, like candy.

ARCTIC OCEAN

A   B   C   D

1

ALASKA
(U.S.A.)

2

YUKON
TERRITORY

NORTHWEST
TERRITORIES

NUNAVUT

PACIFIC
OCEAN

3

Cariboo
Mountains

Hudson
Bay

BRITISH
COLUMBIA

ALBERTA

SASKATCH-
EWAN

MANITOBA

Edmonton

Lake Louise

4

Vancouver
Victoria

Calgary

Saskatoon

ONTARIO

Winnipeg

International Boundary

State Boundary

Arctic Circle

■ **Capital**

● **City**

River

Great
Lakes

5

UNITED STATES

Niagara Falls

Toro

CANADA

GREENLAND
(Denmark)

Arctic Circle

ATLANTIC
OCEAN

N E W F O U N D L A N D

QUEBEC

St. Lawrence River

Gaspé
Peninsula

Quebec

Montreal

NEW
BRUNSWICK

Ottawa

Appalachian
Mountains

PRINCE
EDWARD
ISLAND

NOVA SCOTIA

Horseshoe Falls

N

Alaska A2
Alberta B3
Appalachian
  Mountains
  E5
Arctic Ocean B1
Atlantic Ocean F3

British Columbia A3

Calgary B4
Cariboo Mountains
  B3
Coastal Mountains
  A3–A4

Edmonton B4

Gaspé Peninsula E4
Great Lakes D5
Greenland F1

Horseshoe Falls E5
Hudson Bay D3

Louise, Lake B4

Manitoba C4
Montreal E5

New Brunswick E5
Newfoundland E3–F3
Niagara Falls D5

Northwest
  Territories B3
Nova Scotia F5
Nunavut C3

Ontario D4
Ottawa E5

Pacific Ocean A3
Prince Edward
  Island F5

Quebec E4
Quebec City E5

Rocky Mountains
  A2–B4

St. Lawrence River
  E5
Saskatchewan C3
Saskatoon C4

Toronto E5

United States A5–E5

Vancouver A4
Victoria A4

Winnipeg C4

Yukon Territory A2

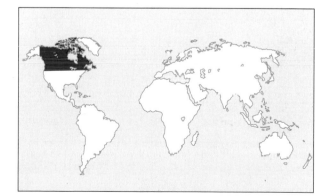

Quick Facts

Land Area	3,849,674 square miles/9,973,249 sq. km
Highest Point	Mount Logan (19,525 feet/5,951 m)
Largest Lake	Lake Superior (31,690 square miles/ 82,100 sq. km)
Longest River	Mackenzie River, Northwest Territories
Population	29,114,000 (1995 census)
Capital	Ottawa
Provinces	Alberta, British Columbia, Manitoba, New Brunswick, Newfoundland, Nova Scotia, Ontario, Prince Edward Island, Quebec, Saskatchewan
Territories	Northwest, Nunavut, Yukon
Major Religions	Anglicanism, Buddhism, Catholicism, Islam
Official Languages	English and French
Major Festivals	Canada Day, July 1
	Thanksgiving, second Monday in October
	Victoria Day, fourth Monday in May
National Symbols	Beaver, Canada Goose, Red Maple
Currency	Canadian dollar (CAN $1.52 = U.S. $1 in 1999)

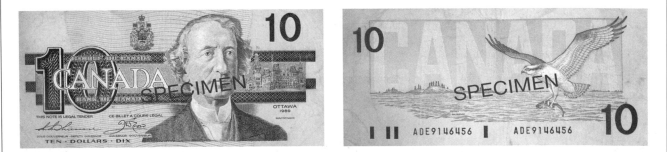

Opposite: Lake Louise in Banff National Park, Alberta.

Glossary

baggataway (ba-gat-teh-WAY): a native game played using a stick and a ball.

ballads: slow, romantic dance songs written in the form of poems.

blubber: the fat of large sea mammals.

camouflage (v): to blend in with the surroundings or habitat.

chuckwagon: a wooden cart that cowboys used on the open range.

colonies: territories within a country that are ruled by another country.

confederation: a group of provinces or states that form an alliance.

convert: to change from one religion to another.

descendants: children of ancestors.

dialect: a special kind of language that is spoken in a particular region of a country.

export: to send out of a country.

fiddleheads: young shoots of ferns. They are eaten in New Brunswick.

fjord: a long, narrow, rocky pass.

immigrants: people who move to a new country and settle there.

insulating material: a fiber that prevents heat from escaping from a room or building.

Inuit: a native tribe of Asian descendants living in North America.

lecture: a school or university class on a particular subject.

Métis: descendants of the original French explorers.

proposal: an offer or suggestion.

rebellions: uprisings against the government or the law.

rivalry: two or more people trying to equal or better one another.

soapstone: a soft stone that feels like soap and is good for carving.

tortiere (tor-tee-EHR): a kind of meat pie made of pork from Quebec.

treaty: an agreement made between two countries.

Vikings: boat travelers from northern Europe who invaded other countries.

More Books to Read

Akavak: An Inuit Eskimo Legend. James A. Houston (Harcourt Brace)

Before the Gold Rush: The Great Klondike Gold Rush. Adventures in Canadian History series. Pierre Berton (McClelland & Stewart)

Calgary Stampede. Patrick Tivy (Altitude Publishing Ltd)

Canada. John Sylvester (Raintree Steck-Vaughn)

Children of the Yukon. Ted Harrison (Tundra Books)

Festivals of the World. Canada. Bob Barlas and Norm Tompsett (Gareth Stevens)

The French Canadian. Nancy Wartik (Chelsea House Publications)

Inuit Art: An Introduction. Ingo Hessel & Dieter Hessel (Harry N. Abrams)

Jacques Cartier, Samuel de Champlain and the Explorers of Canada. Tony Coulter (Chelsea House)

Postcards From Canada. Zoe Dawson (Raintree Steck-Vaughn)

Videos

Call of the Rockies. (National Appraisal and Consulting Association)

Canada. On Top of the World series. (World Life Video Productions)

Canadian Rockies. (Acorn Media Publishing)

Eastern Canada. (National Appraisal and Consulting Association)

Web Sites

www.canada.gc.ca/Canadians/

www.northernlife.com/index.html

www.infocan.gc.ca/facts/index/

www.nlc-bnc.ca/ehome.html

Due to the dynamic nature of the Internet, some web sites stay current longer than others. To find additional web sites, use reliable search engines with one or more of the following keywords to help you locate information on Canada: *Donovan Bailey, Canadian history, Terry Fox, Inuit, Niagara Falls, Quebec, Yukon.*

Index

Alberta 13, 19, 21
Atwood, Margaret 29

Bailey, Donovan 37
ballet 32, 33
Bell, Alexander
    Graham 14
Bondar, Roberta 15
British Columbia 21, 30

Calgary 39
Calgary Stampede 39
Canada goose 5, 9
Canadian Shield 7
Carr, Emily 30
Cartier, Jacques 14
chuckwagons 39
Chute-Montmorency
    Falls 7

dance 33
de Champlain, Samuel
    10

education 24, 25, 28
Ericson, Leif 10

festivals 31, 38, 39
Fox, Terry 25
fur trade 10, 11

Gaspé Peninsula 14
gold rush 13
Great Plains (prairies)
    13

immigrants 21, 27, 28
Inuit (*see* native people)

Klondike 13

lacrosse 37

Macdonald, Sir John A.
    12, 14
Manitoba 19, 21
maple syrup 40, 41
Micmac Indians
    (*see* native people)
Montreal 14, 23, 26, 31

National Hockey league
    (NHL) 36
National Theater
    School 31
native people 10, 20, 21,
    26, 29, 30, 37, 40
New Brunswick 20, 41
Newfoundland 6, 10,
    13, 41
Niagara Falls 6, 7

North American Free
    Trade Agreement
    (NAFTA) 18
Northwest Territories 12
Nova Scotia 20
Nunavut 17, 20

Ondaatje, Michael 29
Ontario 14, 21, 31
Ottawa 16, 17, 30, 38

Prince Edward Island
    29, 40

Riel, Louis 12, 13
Rocky Mountains 7, 34
Royal Canadian Mounted
    Police (RCMP) 12

Saskatchewan 13, 19,
    21, 41
sports 34, 36, 37
Stratford Festival 31

Toronto 24, 27

Vancouver 21
Vikings 10

Yukon 6, 13